FIELD OF LOVE

WITHOUT THIS THOUGHT...
WHO AM I?

MARTIN BIRRITTELLA

ALSO BY MARTIN BIRRITTELLA

Field of Love: Power, Love & Fortune on the Road to Enlightenment – A True Story

Field of Love: How to Experience the Field

Field of Love: Self-Inquiry and the FREE Process Workbook

Please visit:
www.MartinBirrittella.com
www.FieldofLoveBook.com

WITHOUT THIS THOUGHT...
WHO AM I?

FIELD OF LOVE

WITHOUT THIS THOUGHT...
WHO AM I?

MARTIN BIRRITTELLA

Delhi International Press

Copyright© 2013 by Martin Birrittella. All Rights reserved.

No part of this book may be reproduced by any mechanical, photographic, or electronic process, or in the form of a photographic recording; nor may it be stored in a retrieval system, transmitted, or otherwise copied for public or private use—other than for "fair use" as brief quotations embodied in articles and reviews—without prior written permission of the publisher.

The author of this book does not dispense medical advice or prescribe the use of any technique as a form of treatment for physical, emotional or medical problems without the advice of a physician, either directly or indirectly. The intent of the author is only to offer information of a general nature to help you in your quest for emotional and spiritual well-being. In the event you use any of the information in this book for yourself, which is your constitutional right, the author and the publisher assume no responsibility for your actions.

Published in the United States by Delhi International Press Library of Congress Cataloging-in-Publication Data Birrittella, Martin

Field of Love: Without This Thought Who am I?
ISBN 978-0-9899764-8-0 (international trade paper)
ISBN 978-0-9899764-9-7 (kindle ebook)
1. Spiritual 2.Self-Help 3.Personal Growth 1.Title

To you
the Field of Love

WITHOUT THIS THOUGHT...
WHO AM I?

Contents

Self-Inquiry 10
Who Am I? 13
The Free Process 21
    The FREE Process™ 26
    Identify Any Thought. 27
    Consider The Payoffs 28
    Experience & Express the Feelings Associated
        with the Thought 29
    Enlighten & Contemplate 30
The Buddha and the "I" 31
How to Do It 40
    Find 48
    Reveal 50
    Experience & Express 54
    Enlighten & Contemplate 62
    Radical Truth 69

Self-Inquiry

Self-inquiry creates the constant attention to the inner awareness of "I" (or "I am"). To understand the practice of self-inquiry, I believe it's extremely valuable to take a look at the life and teachings of Ramana Maharshi. Ramana was a great Indian sage who expounded self-inquiry in its purest form. He could very well be the reason for self-inquiry's popularity in the 20th and 21st centuries. He taught that the "I" thought disappears and only "Self" awareness remains when you do self-inquiry. The self-inquiry practice Ramana would advise people to do was to simply ask oneself the question, "Who am I?" This practice has become the *sine qua non* of self-inquiry. He said it was the most efficient and direct way of discovering the unreality of any "I" thought. The result of this practice is self realization or liberation.

Much insight can be gained from understanding the life and experiences of Ramana Maharishi. "What we find in the life and teachings of Sri Ramana is the purest of India... He is the whitest spot in a white space," said psychologist Carl Jung. Ken Wilber, noted writer and lecturer called Ramana "the greatest sage of the 20th century."

At the age of 16 Ramana had a transcendent experience which totally transformed his life. We could say he had an unqualified, unbroken experience of the "Field of Love," as I would call it. From then until his death at age 70, Ramana was not only immersed in the awareness of the field, he *was* the field. He radiated the field. Thousands upon thousands of people who went to see him would attest to this. His impact was so broad and wide that even today almost every single teacher of self-inquiry and *Advaita Vedanta* worldwide comes from a connection to him.

Ramana left home following his transcendent experience to live in a very holy site in southern India, Tiruvanamalai. He was inexplicably attracted to the sacred mountain Arunachala. Arunachala overlooks Tiruvanamlai and is worshiped by millions of Hindus as the embodiment of Shiva: otherwise known as the self, or pure awareness.

Ramana was in such an altered state of consciousness when he first arrived in Tiruvanamalai he found a very small 5x5 stone enclosure underneath the massive Shiva temple at the foot of the mountain and he stayed in this enclosure for a number of weeks without moving. This was because he was in a super-conscious state: not eating, drinking, or sleeping—a state which could look like suspended animation but is actually referred to as *Nirvakalpa samadhi*. In this ecstatic state there was no subject or object in his awareness. This even included awareness of his body—and because of this, he was oblivious to the fact that insects were eating through his legs. Some worshipers at the temple found him and pulled him out of the underground enclosure. They put food in his mouth to make him eat. For a short while he wandered naked, completely unaware of his body. This was during the time of British rule. People recognized his extraordinary state and put clothes on him so that the British police would not arrest him.

After a year or so he moved up the side of the mountain and lived in a cave. There, for a period of almost 9 years he was almost completely silent. At the age of 19, one of the individuals who stayed close to him compiled answers to 14 questions that he and others had asked him. The short questions and answers were put together in the form of a book which became in English *Who am I?* In Tamil language the title is *NanYar?* This book became the basis for his first teachings on the process of self-inquiry.

Who Am I?

One of the key factors distinguishing the "Who am I?" inquiry from every other spiritual practice or meditation technique is that almost every other spiritual practice necessitates the existence of a subject who meditates on an object. Ramana from his own experience would say these subject/object forms of meditation would not dissolve the "I" because the moment you came out of meditation or one of those deep states of *samadhi,* the mind would immediately rise up in the form of the ego or "I." Obviously he was talking about his own deep direct experience with states in meditation and *Nirvikapla samadhi* in which all identification was lost.

Ramana said that a yogi could go into a transcendent state of *samadhi,* barely breathing for 21 days—but the moment they came out of it the mind would begin to think and identify subject and object. He stated:

> "Inquiry in the form 'Who am I' alone is the principal means. To make the mind subside, there is no adequate means other than self-inquiry. If controlled by other means, the mind will remain as if subsided, but will rise again."[1]

Ramana referred to the ultimate reality as the heart, or the Self. He would frequently use the Sanskrit term *hridayam* to talk about this center point of the Self. This is not the physical heart nor the heart chakra. It can be translated as the "heart," but a more literal term for the translation of this point is the word "center." Ramana was clear there was not a particular location or center for the Self or heart, but said this point was the source from which all appearances manifested. From a quantum standpoint this center appears to come into being only when it is observed. It is everywhere, like the parts of a holgraphic image, and not subject to time. It is from this heart or center point that all of reality appears.

> *The Heart is another name for the reality and it is neither inside or outside the body. There can be no in or out for it, since it alone is.*[2]

---

1 *Nan Yar?* or *Who am I?* by Sri Ramana as reproduced in the book, *Path of Sri Ramana*, Part One, Fifth Edition. Page 149, 152.
2 D. Mudaliar, op. cit., p.229

The point from which both the heart and reality manifests can be traced to its source simply focusing on the "I" thought.

> "That which rises as 'I' in this body is the mind. If one inquires as to where in the body the thought 'I' rises first, one would discover that it rises in the heart. That is the place of the mind's origin. Even if one thinks constantly 'I','I', one will be led to that place. Of all the thoughts that arise in the mind, the 'I' thought is the first. It is only after the rise of this that the other thoughts arise. It is after the appearance of the first personal pronoun that the second and third personal pronouns appear; without the first personal pronoun there will not be the second and third. The manifestation of physical reality would not come into being until the 'I' thought arose and then everything else is created."[3]

From this statement we can understand that the main payoff we get for any thought is separation. We, the perceiver, separate ourselves from what we perceive. The brain and mind separate subject from the object of thought. The mind instantaneously and very naturally creates separation and duality moment to moment. It is what it does. We innocently disconnect ourselves from our true nature which is pure awareness.

---
3   *Nan Yar?* or *Who am I?* by Ramana Maharshi

Metaphorically our original "I" thought is just like the first domino in an infinite line of interconnected dominoes which are in turn connected to other lines. Once that first domino falls all the other dominoes cannot help but fall, thereby releasing power and creating the movement of reality that we perceive as real.

The dominoes are analogous to our thoughts. Our thoughts connect or attach to one another and a whole series of thoughts and beliefs get supported and come into existence once a second or third person pronoun is conceived in the mind. In fact, the whole world comes into existence.

This is why it is so important in self-inquiry and in using "Who am I?" to find and connect with the original "I" thought and the place or source from where it arises. It also explains why doing inquiry practices where the second and third person objects in a thought or string of thoughts stay alive perpetuates the illusion that everything (including our own separate self, ego, or "I") is real.

Ramana said that meditation practices of subject and object would quiet the mind and they could even produce blissful experiences, *samadhi*, temporary union and merger with subject and object. However, the endpoint (which was his sole interest), would only culminate when the "I" thought was isolated and deprived of its identity.

> "Whence does the 'I' arise? Seek this within then 'I' vanishes. This is the purest wisdom."[4]

This self-inquiry using "Who am I?" to find the source and eliminate the "I" is not the same as the *Soham* mantra. *Soham* is translated as "I am that" or "I am he," subject and object—so this self-inquiry or *vichara* (a sanskrit term), that Ramana taught was clearly different. This is because the *"that"* in *"I am that"* is a second person object. Referring to "I" or "aham" which is the same *aham* in both *soham* "I am that or he" or *koham* "Who am I?"

Ramana stated:

> "Why should we go on saying soham? One must find out the real 'I'. In the question, 'who am I?', 'I' refers to the ego. Trying to trace it and find its source, we see it has no separate existence but merges in the real 'I'."[5]

However, many *Advaita Vedanta* (non-dualistic) teachers of today teach a similar philosophy which has flourished for well over a thousand years. Ramana's "Who am I?" practice is clearly different. *Advaita Vedanta* for the most part recommends a system to mentally or intuitively affirm that the Self is the only reality.

As may be expected, inquiry in the form of "Who am I?" was difficult for many seekers to comprehend.

---

4   Ramana verse 19 "Upadesa Undiyar"
5   D. Mudaliar, op. cit., p.72

Dissolve the "I" using "Who am I?" as an inquiry? For the most part, Ramana sat peacefully day and night in the same location, same room, same sofa with people around him day and night. 24/7. Whenever somebody would ask him a question he would normally say to the questioner, "From where did that thought arise?" The questioner's answer almost always would be: "From me." Ramana would then respond, "Who is that 'me' or 'I'? Inquire into that I and find its source." He was relentless in teaching this way to force the individual to do the practice. People had endless questions about meditation techniques, practices, rebirth, karma, souls, *samadhi*, etc. Sometimes he answered these questions—and when he did, he would immediately then ask the questioner, "From where or from whom did that thought arise?" to put them back into the inquiry practice.

The ultimate reality, the heart (and as I would say, the "Field of Love" is apparent and real on all levels of consciousness whether sleeping, dreaming, or waking. Ramana would comment, *"What is the sense of going after something which was not the ultimate truth during all states of awareness?"* He would say that the heart or Self was the underlying reality which supported the appearance of these three states of awareness. He insisted that it was possible to be aware even during deep sleep. Sometimes he would tell certain individuals to try and find who is there in one's deep sleep state.

Ramana would refer to the Self or this pure awareness as *Turiya*. *Turiya* is also described as the fourth state which is beyond waking, dreaming, and sleeping. It's the name for the state in which you, the individual, are functioning as pure awareness with no "I" or ego remaining. Through science we also know from brain scans that when an individual is in deep sleep the brain neurons are still firing on and off. During this stage the eye movements stop and our brain waves become slower, with occasional bursts of rapid waves called sleep spindles. These are neurons firing on and off but not long enough to communicate with one another. Then delta waves begin to appear which are extremely slow brain waves interspersed with smaller, faster waves—again neurons firing on and off. Ramana would say in *Turiya*, "awareness" is watching but there is absolutely no thought. Scientifically it is now easier to comprehend how this is possible (but difficult to experience).

As with the other practices that I have written about in *Field of Love: How to Experience the Field*, self-inquiry is a very powerful practice. It can be done at any time in any place just by using the inquiry, "Who am I?" Or in thinking, "From where did that thought arise?," and tracing it to its source. When we find that source, we recognize the Field of Love which is around and within us 100% of the time.

Analyzing self-inquiry in regard to the brain and what might be going on when you trace the "I" to its source is fascinating. Alpha theta neuro feedback has you focus on a feedback tone as well as breathing. The brain is literally watching itself go from a fast wave to a slower and slower wave until it reaches theta state (which correlates with deep relaxation and non-REM sleep). Remember Ramana's point, that you can be totally cognizant in deep sleep with no thought. This corresponds to the delta state which is below theta. Inquiring or searching for the "I" and its source appears to naturally take us deeper and deeper, as does slow wave training—because the brain and the mind become very still. Two other benefits that this research has uncovered is that as you drop initially down into a deeper state your glands can be stimulated to release Beta-endorphin and dopamine. In addition to lowering the brain frequency to relax the listener, people going into this very relaxed, deep state reported recalling repressed memories of childhood events. They experienced themselves almost reliving these events as they watched from this deep relaxed state as a witness. Self-inquiry is a great way to find and connect with your heart center or source. The next way I encourage people to access the field is using our innate simple feeling abilities as a catalyst to loosen up our repressed memories when we inquire.

The FREE Process

The FREE Process™ is a self-inquiry technique used to access the Field of Love. The practice combines the 19th century sage Ramana Maharshi's most essential question, "Who am I?" with the simple precursor, "Without this thought," along with deep feeling questions to release the unconscious mind's attachment to a thought. The FREE Process helps us examine each of our thoughts, demands, and beliefs by meeting them with the question, "Without this thought, who am I?" It should not be lost that the essence of the FREE Process is the inquiry "Who am I?" Until the mind completely sinks into its source or its center (the Heart), the work of the inquiry is not done. Writing down thoughts, and investigating the payoffs and feelings one gets for having the thought, and even asking "Without the thought," are all preliminary to engaging the body, brain, and mind so that it is ripe for "Who am I?"

Unlike other forms of inquiry, the FREE Process does not support duality in any way. It solely focuses on the thought, where it is arising from, the feelings associated with it, and who you are without any thought at all. The method employed by Ken Keyes Jr. and Penny Keyes in their book *Handbook to Higher Consciousness The Workbook* has you write down and recognize the payoffs you get for having a demand or belief. You then consciously reprogram your thinking, demands, and beliefs. Although effective, this can still ultimately lead to a sense of separateness because the object of your thought or demand (along with your "I") creates the sense of duality that stays alive in one's mind. This also remains true when the Keyes suggest you combine this exercise with their "instant consciousness doubler" exercise of "experiencing everything that everyone does or says as though you had said or done it." This is very similar to The Work® of Byron Katie in which the inquirer uses turnarounds or reversals when questioning a thought. There are no turnarounds or reversals when using the FREE Process, because subject and object still remain when you put any thought into a second or third person turnaround. Second or third person statements can be very helpful because they can connect you in a deep way to the object of your thought, but in the end they support duality and the sense of separation. This was Ramana's clear statement regarding this:

> "If the first person, I, exists, then the second and third persons, you and he, will also exist. By inquiring into the nature of the I, the I

perishes. With it 'you' and 'he' also perish. The resultant state, which shines as Absolute Being, is one's own natural state, the Self." [6]

Even constructing a thought so that the entire thought is in the first person, (i.e. "I saw myself over there") still supports duality on a subtle level. I wholeheartedly encourage people to do other inquiry practices if they feel so inclined. Even though they can support duality, in the end they can be very effective in helping people let go of stressful thoughts, demands, and beliefs until they arise again—which they are likely to do.

Cognitive Behavioral Therapy or CBT is another form of inquiry or therapy. It has been around for more than 50 years and has been scientifically proven in hundreds of trials to be effective for numerous disorders. Unlike traditional forms of psychotherapy, CBT is focused on the present and is more problem-solving oriented. Like the Keyes' or Byron Katie's related methods it entails identifying distorted thinking, modifying beliefs, relating to others in different ways, and changing behaviors. These techniques are about recognizing what your thoughts and beliefs create within you and what it would be like if you reprogrammed, changed, or let go of these stressful thoughts or beliefs.

The FREE Process simply facilitates the merging of all thought in the heart of the individual. It is best

---

[6] Ramana Maharshi verse 14, *"Reality in Forty Verses"*

suited for those who have done significant meditation, spiritual practice, or other forms of inquiry. Ramana Maharshi clearly stated this in his writing titled *Spiritual Instruction*. When referring to self-inquiry he wrote, "This is suitable only for the ripe souls. The rest should follow different methods according to the state of their minds." The reason inquiry can be difficult is because the practitioner is instructed to inquire into each and every thought no matter what the thought, and to hold one's awareness in the heart space 100% of the time. Ramana said:

> "Gradually one should, by all possible means, try always to be aware of the Self. Everything is achieved if one succeeds in this. Let not the mind be diverted to any other object."

These other methods are for the most part dealing with stressful thoughts and reprogramming the thought process. The goal of the FREE Process is to completely dissolve or eliminate the "I" altogether. In my book, *Field of Love: How to Experience the Field* there are a number of other practices I greatly support and encourage that are not based in eliminating the "I." The basic core of the FREE process is difficult for many people to grasp initially because it challenges the ego and the "I" thought itself. There is a funny cartoon of someone meditating that correlates to this. The caption reads: *"It's all fun and games until someone loses an "I."*

The core of the FREE Process is the recognition that each and every thought we have, no matter how beautiful, positive, loving, or transcendent creates a sense of separation. This is the primary payoff we get for having any thought, and identifying as the "I," mind, or thinker of that thought. This is what distinguishes this method of inquiry from other methods that support the sense of "I" and the objects and thoughts that are arising, investigated, and inquired into.

Even if you "release" or "let go" there is still a sense that the object that was "let go of" or "released" is real, existent and separate. Experiencing and expressing before inquiring, "Without this thought, who am I?", is key to having the FREE Process work. The next 4 boxes simplifies the FREE Process. A more in-depth analysis along with examples of the FREE Process are discussed in subsequent chapters.

WITHOUT THIS THOUGHT,
WHO AM I?

The FREE Process™

Find & Reveal:
- Identify every thought.

Experience & Express:
- Consider the payoffs you get for having the thought.
- Experience and express the feelings associated with the thought.

Enlighten & Contemplate:
- Inquire: "Without this thought, *Who am I?*"

Identify Every Thought

- I am _____

- He / she / they are _____

- It is _____

- What do you want? _____

- Not want? _____

- How do you feel he / she / you / it should be?
  _____

- Or shouldn't be? _____

- What do you want him / her / you / it to be? Or not be?
  _____

Inspired by the *Handbook to Higher Consciousness The Workbook* by Ken Keyes, Jr. and Penny Keyes. © 1989

Consider The Payoffs

- I feel separate.
- I feel superior.
- I feel happy, joyful, ecstatic.
- I feel less than or inferior.
- I feel sorry for myself.
- I disconnect myself from the object (person or thing) of my thought.
- I support my belief that the object of my thought is real.

Additional payoffs:

- I get to be right and make the other person wrong. I can avoid looking at "what is" in my life.
- I'll prove it's unfair or untrue.
- I get attention, sympathy, agreement, approval, and/or comfort.

- It feels safe to keep a distance from other people (or a specific person). I avoid taking responsibility for what I do, say, or feel.

- I don't have to really experience what I am feeling.

- People will know that I'm (a good teacher, a responsible parent, A caring person, a skilled bricklayer, etc.)

- People won't think I'm (egotistical, a coward, etc.). I have an excuse for poor performance.

- I get to avoid confronting the addictions that would come up if I weren't running this addiction.

- It feels safe and familiar to hold onto the old pattern, and scary to let go. I get to play martyr.

- I get to play the victim role.

Inspired by the *Handbook to Higher Consciousness The Workbook* by Ken Keyes, Jr. and Penny Keyes. © 1989

Experience & Express the Feelings Associated with the Thought

Experience

- How do I feel when I have this thought?
- How do I physically feel when I have this thought?
- Where in my body do I feel it?
- How do I feel about the object of this thought (person or thing) when I have the thought?
- How do I treat the object of this thought when they are in front of me?
- How do I treat the object of this thought in my mind?
- What do I think of them, how do I see them?

Express

- If I do not suppress or censor myself in any way, what do I want to express in association with this thought?
- Get honest, let it out.

Enlighten & Contemplate

■ **INQUIRE:**

■ **Without this thought, *Who am I?***

The Buddha and the "I"

The single biggest block to expanded awareness is the thought "I am the body." The Buddha taught that from the highest spiritual standpoint, the concept of "I" is an illusion. He said that there is no reason to think that there is a soul that comes from another world or realm that will transmigrate to another realm after death. To the Buddha everything was an illusion created within the mind. It was radical at the time for the Buddha to say that the "I," the soul, was not real. The Buddha recognized if the "I" and/or the soul was not real then all of the other objects perceived by that individual were not real as well. This was the heart and the essence of the Buddha's *Anatta* doctrine. The Buddha recommended that seekers not waste time, and just focus on finding peace and happiness in this moment by recognizing that everything is not real. It is all an illusion, and the mind experiences suffering because it thinks its body and the objects around it are real. Because of the teachings of Ramana and the Buddha the first thoughts I prompt people to inquire about are their bodies, mind, and even their belief in their soul. These are the biggest illusions our brains and minds are convinced are real. Ramana stated many times:

> "The mind is nothing else than the 'I'-thought. The mind and the ego are one and the same. Intellect, will, ego, and individuality are collectively the same mind.[7]"

The next thoughts to inquire about are the people closest to you: mother, father, etc., which are also a powerful illusions that most of us are dearly and emotionally attached to. You can then move on to everyone, everything and every thought that arises.

The FREE Process calls on the inquisitive nature of the mind as a tool to untangle its hold on our identification as separate individual egos with a physical body because everyone reports "I am," "I feel," etc. In other words, the "I" is real and no one doubts or questions that.

We can deduce from the findings of brain science that the sense of "I" only exists when a mammal's frontal lobe has enough neurons for it to generate the "I" thought. Does a field mouse have the sense of "I"? A cat, a dog? A newborn infant? At what point does the sense of "I" arise? We do know that anyone reading this has the sense of "I" arising within. There are approximately 150,000,000,000 neurons constantly firing on and off in our brain to create the appearance

---

7 Ramana Maharshi *Self-Inquiry*

of separation between ourselves and all the objects around us. People who have had a near death experience or out-of-body experience will tell you that there is a sense of non-separation during the event, but as soon as it wears off the brain does its job of separating and making sure we don't walk off a cliff or walk into on-coming traffic.

Many hidden beliefs can be stored in the mind and body. Deeply unconscious thoughts can be sparked by unusual events. I had back surgery at the age of forty-eight that acted as the trigger to unearth the unconscious belief that I was not lovable and consequently had to take total care and responsibility for my own well -being. For my entire adult life, I did not have a clue that I was holding on to this thought so strongly on an unconscious level. The experience showed me how difficult it can be to uproot unconscious impressions that often have a more powerful hold on us than conscious impressions. This was true for me even though I had been meditating for over 30 years. I wanted to find a simple, direct way to unearth and work through my most fundamental unconscious beliefs, and so I started pushing myself to question all my thoughts from a deep feeling perspective to see what would arise.

The idea that I was "not lovable" had been stored in me for decades, and there apparently was a part of me that did not want to let it go. I discovered that the thought protected me with a false belief that if I completely took care of myself, I wouldn't have to rely on anyone. In fact, I had a tendency to flat out refuse receiving help. My brain and senses automatically created this separation both to keep me safe in the world and to motivate me into action so I could be the one in charge.

We have numerous unconscious, subconscious, and repressed memories that are stored in the brain—some would say even in our cells or in our subtle bodies. These thoughts, beliefs, and memories are like the files on a computer. The Hindu yogis called these stored impressions *samskaras* and *vasanas*. They explain that they come from events in this life and from past lives. According to them these impressions are stored in the subtle body, the chakras or energy centers, and the central subtle nerve within the spine called the *sushumna*. These memories, impressions, *vasanas* and *samskaras* keep us from connecting and accessing the field all around us. Brain scientists conclude that memories are neurologically imprinted in us, and the body and psyche have memorized many of them so incredibly well that we don't consciously recognize them.

These impressions are so embedded that trying to think our way out of an unconscious belief using the conscious mind doesn't work most of the time. Exactly how these are recorded by neurons within the brain scientists don't know other than seeing what areas of the brain are active when prompted to think or move a certain way. This is why people might do things like primal therapy, for example, in order to loosen up, discover, and release these stored feelings and beliefs. Scientific evidence shows the subconscious mind reacts faster and is larger than the conscious mind and accounts for over 90% of the brain's activity every day.

What is even more amazing to consider is that our brain and minds appear to be acting somewhat independently of our conscious cognitive will. The synopsis of a paper published in *Nature Neuroscience* by Chun Siong Soon, Marcel Brass, Hans-Jochen Heinze and John-Dylan Haynes, entitled *"Unconscious determinants of free decisions in the human brain"* was: "There has been a long controversy as to whether subjectively 'free' decisions are determined by brain activity ahead of time. We found that the outcome of a decision can be encoded in brain activity of prefrontal and parietal cortex up to 10 seconds before it enters awareness. This delay presumably reflects the operation of a network of high-level control areas that begin to prepare an upcoming decision long before it enters awareness." The well known philosopher, teacher and author Dr. David Hawkins writes:

> *"We take subjectivity for granted. We take the Field for granted. We take consciousness for granted... [Yet] this is what we are. We ignore what we are in return for focusing on that which we are not. At this very instant, 99% of your mind is silent... The reason you don't notice it is because you're focused on*

the 1% that's noisy. It's like you have a vast amphitheatre—let's take a great ballpark that seats forty, a hundred thousand people. Nobody's there, middle of the night, but over in the corner there's one little tiny transistor radio, one four-inch TV, and that's what you're focused on... You think this is where the action is, you're focused on the little tiny thing of the moment attracting your attention. Because attention is focused here, you think that's what your mind is. That's not what your mind is. Your mind is the Absolute Silence. If your mind wasn't silent, you wouldn't know what you were thinking about. If it wasn't for the silence in the woods, you couldn't hear any noise. How could you hear a bird sing? It's only against the background of silence. It's only against the background of the innate silence of the mind that you can witness what the mind is thinking about. At that realization you call it 'it' instead of 'me'. It's not what my mind is thinking about, it's what it is thinking about." Dr. David Hawkins, M.D., Ph.D., *The Highest Level of Enlightenment*

He also states in his book *Power Versus Force: The Hidden Determinants of Human Behavior:* "We think we live by forces we control, but in fact we are governed by power from unrevealed sources, power over which we have no control."

Much of the activity, movement, and release of our unconscious is also governed by this same pre-determined force. This is why one of the primary lessons I insist upon is to be kind to oneself at all times. You can understand why inquiry, or any meditation technique, can be difficult because they all have to deal with these powerful predetermined forces.

This research and statement are amazing concepts when you consider that we think our conscious mind is making decisions moment to moment before we act, when in fact the majority of the impetus is coming from our *unconscious*. It also supports my experience that what is happening is all movement and we fool ourselves into thinking we are the doer. You can also understand why it might be silly to believe we know everything—especially about ourselves, our minds, our emotions. This also supports noted quantum physicist, David Bohm's theory which he writes about in his book, *Thought as a System*. He speaks eloquently about the interconnected instantaneous reflexive nature of thought, the brain, mind, feeling, emotion, and the body. The key word here is *reflexive*. We all know what happens when a doctor taps us on the knee. It moves—it does not have a choice. Is the same thing happening with our thoughts and feelings? I say yes. My point here for emphasis, is that it is important to move our attention and awareness continuously (and uninterruptedly, if possible) when doing spiritual practice—and self-inquiry in particular, because reality is so spontaneously reflective of the events (including our thoughts and feelings), that preceded them.

The FREE Process is designed to connect any arising thought and stimulate the unconscious thoughts and beliefs that could be underlying it. We do this by engaging the thought with deep feeling probing questions to unlock its connection to other thoughts, feelings, and beliefs in the unconscious mind. This process can release a whole range of feelings from sadness, euphoria, anger, love, and anxiety, in addition to other thoughts. To follow the computer analogy, it is not enough to look at the titles of files (thoughts) stored in the computer and try to delete them. Some inquiry methods would simple say *"release"* the thoughts when you recognize them arising on the screen of your mind. My experience is that we must click on the thought file, open it up, and let it play in the mind and heart, feeling it with full expression. You have to totally *feel* the thoughts arising in the mind and see how they affect you so that the unconscious beliefs connected with them, or supporting them at the root are also revealed. Then a whole series of connected thoughts and feelings that are supporting this belief can be recognized, loosened, investigated, and inquired into, thus allowing them to also be released and dissolved. Getting in touch and recognizing the "payoffs" one gets for having a thought is invaluable in loosening up our attachment to a thought or belief, but it is important to take it one step further and feel and express the feelings associated with the thought, even the positive and joyful ones in order to let go, release, and transcend them by recognizing they are not who we really are.

How to Do It

Here are examples of some personal thoughts of mine. For many years, I had strong beliefs about my mother.

I hate my mother. My mom is a Nazi. My mother didn't support me.

I probed my mind first see what the payoffs were for having these thoughts. The answers: *I separate myself from her. I think I am better and more spiritual than she is. I get to play the victim role. I don't have to experience what I am feeling.*

Then I asked myself some deep feeling questions.

How does it feel to have these thoughts? I sat silently for a moment and allowed myself to feel and experience the answers.

It feels uncomfortable, bad, disturbing. I don't like how it feels at all.

Going even deeper I imagined my mom in my mind's eye.

How do I treat my mom in my mind when I have these thoughts?

My answer: *I distance myself from her every way I can. I want to stop thinking about her. If I think about her I want to attack her in some way to protect myself.*

To really get to the root of my feeling about her I asked myself:

If I did not suppress or censor myself in any way, what do I want or need from my mom?

This is a powerful *feeling* question of the FREE Process because it works to engage the unconscious mind to dig deep into the true feelings that are supporting the thought. If I simply allow myself to feel and express what arises about my mom for just for a moment and get really honest without suppressing or censoring myself—this is what I hear:

I just want my mom to love me. I want my mom to be supportive. I don't want her to judge me.

As I sat quietly with these answers, a feeling of love began to arise in me and I allowed this *feeling* to come out and be *expressed*.

I then inquired into the original thoughts one at a time and listen for the answers.

I hate my mother.

Without the thought, "I hate my mom," who am I?

My mom is a Nazi.

Without the thought, "My mom is a Nazi," who am I?

My mother didn't support me.

Without the thought, "My mother didn't support me," who am I?

I was so committed to the beliefs about my mom that not having those feelings was strange. From a very still, honest point inside my heart, I heard and felt another answer arise:

Without the thoughts about my mom, I would be free, I would be free of a big belief about my mom. In fact, without the thought I can feel myself dissolving, right here, right now and a feeling of intense love arising.

In this process, I recognized I had grown attached to the thought and beliefs about her over time and it permeated the way I treated her in my mind, my actions, and in her presence. I realized that all the negative thoughts about my mother existed to keep me separate from her and safe from the possibility that she, whom I loved so dearly, could hurt me. Even more so it kept me from experiencing my own self love and the Field of Love all around me because being separate felt so safe, so smart and wise to me. It also led me to ask, "without any thought at all," who am I?

Another common example

I hate Tom for abusing me.

Payoffs for having this thought:

I hate myself for allowing his abuse. I hate him and completely distance myself from him. I protect myself from not only him but everyone else who could possibly hurt me.

Feelings connected or associated with this thought: Where do I feel it in my body?

I feel it in my stomach, in my gut. I feel it radiating throughout my whole being.

I feel hatred and contempt for him when I see or think about him.

If I did not censor or suppress myself in any way what do I want from Tom?

I want him to die. I don't ever want to see him again.

It is extremely important to recognize that there is absolutely no judgment to what feelings may arise. It does not matter if you feel furious, angry, sad, loving, happy, or euphoric. The key with the FREE Process is to allow yourself **total freedom** to express what is moving through you. Then and only then should you inquire into the thought.

Now inquire:
"Without the thought 'I hate Tom', who am I?"

Be still and find out who you are without the thought and the feelings attached to it.

These examples of the FREE Process illustrate how effective it can be in releasing both the conscious and unconscious mind. When the root of a thought or belief can clearly be identified, viewed, and expressed with full awareness, it naturally dissolves on its own and merges with the heart or source lying within us. The key is that it does not matter what the feeling associated with the thought is, where and how you are feeling it within the body, and whether it is a **"positive"** or **"negative"** emotion. Just allow yourself to be completely honest and let the feeling to be experienced and expressed. It does not matter what it looks like or sounds like when it comes out. A thought is a thought, and a feeling is a feeling, and you are neither. You are pure awareness.

The goal is to experience yourself as pure awareness without any preconceived judgment whatsoever. It does not matter what it looks, feels, or sounds like. Allowing yourself complete permission to go all the way through this stills the mind, dissolves thought, and merges the object of the thought with the heart or core center of your being. This creates a natural fusion of love and a door to experience the Field.

I purposely used these two examples to show the reader that the feelings and outcome of the payoffs and feelings can be quite different. In the end, no matter what payoffs or feelings arise, the thought is met with, "Without the thought, who am I?"

I strongly encourage people to do the FREE Process on the thoughts and feelings about your body, mind, and soul. This is subtle, but when you do this all thought begins to dissolve, and the result is total merger with the Field of Love. Eventually this will lead you to inquire and question every thought that arises.

Here are examples of thoughts that don't appear connected to our personal self:

Peaches are delicious or *Judy is sweet*. We can inquire into any thought—and should—because all thought has the ability to separate us from our awareness (which is the Field of Love). Ramana was clear that in order to dissolve the "I" completely into the heart you need to inquire into all thought, all the time.

Processing a seemingly benign or even positive thought can seem unnecessary and almost ridiculous.

The reality is that these thoughts are upheld by deep unconscious beliefs that support our whole identification system. Our brains have predetermined what peaches are, what delicious means, who Judy is, and what it is to be sweet. We are so convinced of our beliefs, and what we perceive as absolute truths, that these beliefs permeate ALL of our thoughts from the mundane to the beautiful, and even the insane. This activity of the unconscious mind is what creates the payoffs to keep us separate from the field of pure awareness because our normal awareness has so much confidence in "knowing" and "separating" everything.

The conscious mind taking unconscious beliefs intuitively as fact, uses its cognitive ability to formulate judgments about what people and things *should* or *shouldn't* be doing. It also judges what we personally *should* or *shouldn't* be doing. This brain activity can be troublesome when trying to access the unifying nature of the field. We are working with a loaded deck of beliefs so ingrained that they are almost impossible to overcome. This is the main reason for inquiring continuously into all thought.

In summary, the FREE Process begins by identifying any thought or belief, finding the payoffs the thought creates, and feeling and expressing the feelings associated with the thought before inquiring. The feeling questions we ask can momentarily still the mind and overcome the conscious thinking upper part of the brain. Our cognitive thinking brain is so sure it knows everything. By prompting the thinking brain to feel by asking it questions about "feeling" it naturally lets go and allows our lower more primitive feeling brain to work. *The lower brain is so connected to the body that when you ask it to feel it looks to the body to respond with the answer, whether it be the heart, belly, throat, etc.* In essence we are undermining our cognitive thinking process with these questions. These questions act like disruptive explosive charges to momentarily still the upper thinking "knowing" brain and get our awareness to just feel, so that the thinking brain does not have any support. The reason we do inquiry and the FREE Process is because in reality we are not our brain, mind, thoughts, feelings, or body. We are pure awareness which is utilizing them and creating a sense of "I" and individuality.

When we plant the mind with the these feeling questions, we effectively loosen and stir up the bedrock of our unconscious so that it will not only reveal even deeper thoughts and beliefs hidden below, but also lead us to the experience of who we are without thought, feeling, and everything else attached to it. In the moment we inquire, "Without the thought, who am I?" our cognitive structure is temporarily untethered to past beliefs. The cognitive mind frantically searches for an answer. It searches for itself. It searches for its Source. It literally tries to find itself so that it can reestablish its identity and very existence. While it searches, a new perspective that isn't tethered to what we think we know as absolute "truth" arises as pure awareness, which is our true nature. This could last for a millisecond or go on for a lifetime. This is why Ramana continuously would ask people, "From where did that thought arise?" It leads the mind to pure awareness.

This Source is the same gap that's talked about in meditation, where pure awareness continually resides. This feeling of the gap can be so expanding and transcending that it often alters our perception and experience of reality. We begin to see the benefit not only of letting go of the beliefs and concepts we've clung to, but of ultimately dropping all thoughts, beliefs, or concepts. In other words, we could ask the question, "Without *any* thought, who am I?" or "Letting go of every thought, who am I?" If you inquire into every single thought, eventually everything appears as movement.

All that remains is pure awareness and an experience of the Field of Love.

Find

"FREE" is an acronym to help us understand this process a little better. The "F" in FREE stands for "find." People often ask what thought or belief to work on first. I find it's best to explore our most basic identifications — which are (as I said in the prior chapter): body, mind, and soul. Then I would move on to the people closest to us both emotionally and physically. Finally to food, sex, money, or other pleasures or pains whether they attract or repulse us—as they are natural energetic responses of the lower brain. Many responses that are automatic have developed over millions of years of evolution. Focusing our attention to inquire into the nature of each of these individual objects and desires is what frees the mind from attachment. Go after these basic identifications, needs, wants, desires, or repulsions one by one and inquire into them. The judgments we have about ourselves and others is the most fertile ground. Gradually the entire FREE Process will unfold instantaneously as you watch yourself question every thought that enters your mind.

How much stuff is there to find? Your brain is like a computer that has downloaded everything that has been recorded through your senses for your entire lifetime. It has all the backup proof it needs to determine who, and what you are. Many people who have near death experiences claim that they watched their entire life play back very rapidly. That would be a tremendous amount of information on somebody's hard drive. This internal hard drive plays a big part in our unconscious memory. For this reason when rummaging through our thoughts and beliefs we must go very slowly and carefully, because we don't know what we will find. Be kind to yourself.

We can use the FREE Process on anything that comes to mind, even the most basic or innocuous.

Thoughts can be processed whether they are stressful or pleasurable because they are all connected to the unconscious brain, which supports our conscious belief system. Other methods of inquiry have a tendency to just go after stressful thoughts. Inquiring into pleasant thoughts can be enlightening because we love, support, and are convinced of the truth and accuracy of these thoughts—even more so than stressful thoughts. Example: *I love my husband.* If you love your husband, it is almost impossible at first to inquire or question that thought. It sounds crazy because you are as sure of your love as you are sure of your own self, identity, or "I." The reality is that you can inquire into *I love my husband* and if you get very honest and go deep it is interesting where it takes you and what you find. Stressful thoughts usually attract us first because they are so familiar, cause pain, and we want to get rid of them. Thoughts and beliefs are so ingrained that you will find that the same ones will come up again and again—even after you inquire and get very clear about them. This is natural, and part of the process. Just allow them to come. Don't judge, just inquire again and find out who you are without the thought or belief.

Reveal

The next step in the FREE inquiry process is the "R" that stands for "reveal." This appears at first to be relatively easy, but it can be a little more difficult than one expects. The mind and thought process moves so incredibly fast that even if one finds something to investigate, it will move on to the next thought instantly. It is common knowledge that the mind has tens of thousands of thoughts every day and averages a thought every few seconds. By the time you have a thought it's on to the next. Because of this natural response the mind thinks, "I got this. I can do this quickly. This is a piece of cake, I don't have to write it down." However, it is helpful to write down the thought that you want to inquire about. If you just think it and don't write it down, it is very easy to lose the thought or belief, and be on to the next one that arises in your mind. Byron Katie noted in *Losing The Moon, Byron Katie Dialogues on Non-Duality, Truth and Other Illusions* edited by Ellen J. Mack, "The first year—I say the first three years, but the first few months, whatever it was—I was writing all the time." I think we can take this as a good lesson that writing all the time can be very helpful at first.

Sometimes the unconscious mind immediately recognizes what your cognitive mind is up to when it starts to inquire, and it doesn't like it. This is because it has a sense that it is about to lose something. It hates to lose anything—especially its own identity. Think of the moments you walk past a mirror and purposely don't look. You do that in the moment because it is more peaceful not to look at yourself than look. The instant the mind sees or knows what it is or might get, it immediately wants to control the situation to protect itself. The same is true in inquiry. The mind wants to control everything.

The conscious mind definitely doesn't want to lose its sense of self. After all, it has worked so many years building it up. The other aspect of the revealing process that is valuable, is to have the statements you have written down heard out loud (if it's possible) with a friend who understands this inquiry process.

The reason for this is twofold. First, the actual verbalization and expressing of the thought itself can trigger the additional unconscious beliefs that support the first thought, or it can reveal whole other areas of even more deeply held beliefs to investigate. Secondly, there is a lot of vibrational power in revealing by verbalizing the words of the thought or belief. Hearing the thoughts aloud begins to loosen the protective shield they have lived within, and for someone else to hear and be a witness to them can loosen things further. This is a primary reason people go to therapy and express out loud what is going on with them. The FREE Process works the exact same way. You become your own therapist, asking yourself in the presence of a friend or alone by yourself:

How is it going? What am I thinking? What's the payoff for having that thought? How does it feel to have that thought? If I didn't suppress myself what do I want or need from that person, thing, or me? Can I feel it, express it, and let it out? Finally, Without the thought, who am I?

My experience is that the person you are sharing your thoughts with usually has a strong tendency to be compassionate and kind to you, especially if you take turns doing it with one another.

The person with whom you practice should only bear witness to the thoughts and beliefs you are revealing. That's it. Period. They are not there for judgment or discussion in any way. Let me say that again. The person who is bearing witness and listening to your statements (i.e. I am _____or my body is _____, etc.) should in no way start a discussion on any level about these statements. **This inquiry practice is about you and only you.** It is for you to find both the conscious and unconscious thoughts attached to your statement, the payoffs and feelings associated with the thought—not your friend.

If you practice the FREE Process with someone you are in an intimate relationship with and they are bearing witness to what you have to say about *them*, they have to be willing to be the listener without any judgment. Doing this can be very powerful for both parties, especially the one who is doing the revealing. Again, it is necessary that the person you are practicing with completely understands the FREE process and recognizes that the exercise is intended to free the writer of the thoughts, and not the one who is listening to them. They can have their turn at some point if you both should choose. You may hear some things you never heard before. It takes a special relationship to be able to hear each other's most intimate thoughts and it is absolutely imperative that if the listener cannot do this that they stop the process immediately, for their own benefit.

Listeners should be very sweet to themselves and be sensitive enough to their own inner intuition to recognize what they can and cannot hear. They also must be willing to stop if necessary. This is not easy to do until it is practiced a bit, and one can find their own personal limit. I have done this on many occasions with people with whom I have been in an intimate relationship, and have found it to be extremely healing and freeing. This is especially true if your thoughts are completely uncensored, truthful, and honest. I have also had people say "I can't hear this," or "I can't do this," and we have stopped. Doing that is an absolute must. I honor and respect everyone who recognizes their limits and requests that they not be stretched.

Experience & Express

The first "E" in FREE stands for "Experience and Express."

The first thing we are going to do in "experience" is consider the "payoffs" we get for having a particular thought or belief. Once we are clear about the payoff(s) we get, we are going to use our sense and feeling to investigate honestly into the deepest part of our mind to experience, express, and release the feelings that are associated with each thought.

I like to say *Feel-Feel-Feel* when people ask, "How do I experience?" Feeling is one of the main ingredients of the FREE Process that distinguishes it from other practices. We are naturally disconnected from our own feelings and it does not matter how intelligent or how spiritual or compassionate we perceive ourselves to be. Experience here is all about connecting the higher cognitive thinking brain, which understands the real payoffs for a thought, with the core unconscious brain through feeling. Again, it is important to understand feeling and the implications of allowing ourselves to feel our feelings because they are at the root of and support our cognitive mind. As a society, we have been trained to suppress our feelings. *Repressed* feelings are those that we are completely out of touch with. They are considered repressed because they are unconscious. *Suppressed* feelings, on the other hand, are ones we consciously hold down—for numerous reasons. If we suppress feelings long enough they can become unconscious and repressed. Using inquiry, we are going to try and unlock both suppressed and repressed feelings that are tied to our thoughts in order to find freedom from our thoughts and belief systems.

Depending on our upbringing, three emotions that can be difficult to feel and connect with are sadness, anger, and fear. From the time most of us were very small children, our parents unknowingly taught us how we should react and express these feelings. A sad or troubled child is a real concern for almost every parent, and they naturally want to alleviate their child's pain in any way possible. A parent will pick up a child if they are sad or crying to divert their attention and reassure them with, "Don't be sad—everything is going to be ok." As a result, the child's subconscious learns that it is not good to be sad, and begins to suppress their emotion (energy in motion) in their body and not let it move through naturally. The same is true for anger. A parent might react to their child's rage with, "How dare you talk to me like that!" One of my mom's favorite sayings to me and my six brothers was, "I am going to wash your mouth out with soap if you speak to me like that!" As a young child, these common expressions leave a powerful impact, and we learn to suppress. Even in the face of fear, there is so often no acknowledgement of the root cause. A child may be scared to death about something but is told, "It's ok, there is nothing to be afraid of, put your head down and go back to sleep." All of this conditioning makes it imperative to give ourselves complete permission to feel what is really being held inside when doing the FREE Process, so that we can release it and see what is on the other side of letting go.

Another major problem that many "spiritually inclined" people have is that they tend to believe that expressing anger, sadness, or fear is a sign of weakness, and that not expressing these emotions shows an enlightened self-control. We've come to believe that anger is not a quality a spiritual seeker should show or hold in their heart. It doesn't matter if we are Buddhist, or Christian, etc. Our idea of what it means to be "spiritual" is derived from examples conjured up in our minds of beautiful Buddhist monks dressed in saffron robes with love and compassion on their faces, or of Mother Teresa selflessly serving God. By trying to portray this level of peace without thoroughly investigating our underlying feelings, we are suppressing and supporting the repression of unconscious beliefs and identifications stored in the brain and body. Again, anyone who has experienced therapy understands this, as therapists constantly work with their clients to help them to access such feelings.

I like to use the analogy of a pool of water to describe the predicament of premature peace or compassion. I am going to call this water the "pool of loving compassion." You want to go swimming in this pool but you have a little problem. You are covered in grease. This grease represents all the impressions you have been holding onto for lifetimes: hatred, anger, love, fear, lust, sadness, etc. They are consciously and—more importantly—unconsciously stuck to, or living within you. The reality is that they are there whether you like it or not. Does it make sense to go sit in the pool of compassion and wait a very long time for the grease and grime to dissolve on its own as you "meditate" them away? Would that eventually work, or would it be wiser to remove some of the grease before you get in the water? With inquiry you can do just that by being proactive and allowing and prompting your mind to find suppressed and repressed feelings that are supporting all your thoughts or beliefs.

Another great example of not suppressing strong feelings but letting them arise and come out no matter what it looks like is Jesus. This is a good lesson for all who think that holding down anger, fear, and sadness is a good thing or "the spiritual thing to do." "I will meditate these things away," "I am holding my mind in a transcendent peaceful state." Yes that is true, you are holding your mind in a peaceful state—but what is underneath, in the unconscious?

In the garden of Gethsemane Christ showed how an "enlightened being" dealt with sadness, anger, and fear at his time of anguish. He didn't suppress or censor himself in any way. This is key—and what I encourage individuals to do with the FREE Process.

Christ went to the garden after the last supper with a few of his disciples. They had just had a big Passover meal, and his disciples were tired. He went to pray alone a few yards away from them. Christ had a good sense of what was about to happen. He knew it was going to be painful. He was in great anguish and started to experience deep agony. This is why it is actually referred to as the *Agony in the Garden* in religious literature. In essence, he was scared to death. Matthew,

Mark, and Luke all described this scene in great detail. Here is the account from Mark:

> *They went to a place called Gethsemane, and Jesus said to his disciples, "Sit here while I pray." He took Peter, James and John along with him, and he began to be deeply distressed and troubled. "My soul is overwhelmed with sorrow to the point of death," he said to them. "Stay here and keep watch." Going a little farther, he fell to the ground and prayed that if possible the hour might pass from him. "Abba, Father," he said, "everything is possible for you. Take this cup from me. Yet not what I will, but what you will." Then he returned to his disciples and found them sleeping. "Simon," he said to Peter, "are you asleep? Could you not keep watch for one hour? Watch and pray so that you will not fall into temptation. The spirit is willing, but the body is weak." Once more he went away and prayed the same thing. When he came back, he again found them sleeping, because their eyes were heavy. They did not know what to say to him. Returning the third time, he said to them, "Are you still sleeping and resting? Enough! The hour has come. Look, the Son of Man is betrayed into the hands of sinners. Rise! Let us go! Here comes my betrayer!"*

It's clear that Christ didn't stop himself from expressing his feelings. He had to let them out. He didn't care how he looked. He wasn't thinking, "I am the master, I am the Son of God." He got up and went to his disciples and begged them first to stay awake with him. He came back a second time and was disturbed that they would not stay awake. Finally after a third time he was angry, and gave up trying to get the disciples to stay awake.

Rumi was very succinct in encouraging emotional expression when he wrote:

"Cry out all your grief, your disappointments!"

Like Christ or Rumi, when you are doing this process have no fear of expressing anything moving through you whether it's love, sadness, fear, hate, or anger. Do not suppress, do not censor yourself. Do not care what it looks like. Just feel it, get in touch with it, see what it feels like to have a thought, and what you do to yourself and others when you have it.

The Feeling Questions

- How do I feel when I have this thought?

- How do I physically feel when I have this thought? Where in my body do I feel it?

- How do I feel about the object of this thought (person or thing) when I have this thought?

- How do I treat the object of this thought when they are in front of me? How do I treat the object of this thought in my mind? What do I think of them, how do I see them?

- If I do not suppress or censor myself in any way, what do I want to express in association with this thought?

Remember, the FREE Process is about getting rid of the sense of separation that the "I" (ego) creates with all of the objects around it. The above feeling questions will help you get in touch with your unconscious beliefs and help you release your attachment to your conscious thoughts and beliefs.

Enlighten & Contemplate

Enlightening ourselves is the final part of the FREE Process.

We ask ourselves Ramana Maharishi's question *"Who am I?"* with the precursor, *"Without this thought..."*

"Without this thought, who am I?"

Other forms of the question are:

"Who am I without this thought?"
or
"Letting go of this thought, who am I?"

All of these inquiry questions will take you to the source of the "I."

The key is to just be still and experience the answer to this question.

After you sit with the question, you may then be inclined to ask yourself:

"Without any thought, who am I?"

More helpful examples:

Let's do the complete FREE Process using the following six very different examples to see what it could look and sound like.

We will work on one thought at a time.

We will consider the payoffs for each thought and then ask feeling questions before finally inquiring, **"Without the thought, who am I?"**

1. *I hate my body.*

2. *My soul is divine.*

3. *My mind is driving me crazy.*

4. *My husband is mean to me.*

5. *People shouldn't suffer.*

6. *I love Mike.*

Example 1
I hate my body.

I consider the payoffs I get (on page 28 and page 29). Then I ask myself some feeling questions and these are some sample answers:

I feel pathetic and hopeless. I feel as if I will never be able to change.

I feel as if my body is not good enough, so I ignore it. I won't look at it, and I treat it like a friend whom I'd rather not see, but can't get rid of.

I just want my body to be ok. I don't want it to hassle me in any way. I wish my body could just mind its own business and not be an issue for me. I want my body to leave me alone.

Now Inquire:

Close your eyes, imagine your body in your mind, and ask yourself: **"Without the thought, 'I hate my body', who am I?"**

Just sit with the answer and the feeling or awareness that comes.

It may be stillness, peace, or nothing at all—only quiet. Stay in that space as long as it feels comfortable.

Many thoughts and beliefs are so deep, so rooted in our unconscious, that often it feels unnatural, foreign, and shocking to imagine what it would be like to not have the thought to which we have become so attached and identified. This letting go into pure awareness beyond thought is your true nature. It is the real you.

Example 2
My soul is divine.

I consider the payoffs. There are payoffs for every thought. They may be positive or negative, obvious or subtle. You can have multiple payoffs for the same thought, as the mind moves and examines the payoffs. Then I ask myself some feeling questions. These are some sample answers to the feeling questions:

It feels good to recognize my soul as divine.

I treat my soul with respect and love most of the time.

I wish I could connect more directly with my soul, its purpose, and my divinity.

Now inquire:

Close your eyes, imagine your soul in your mind, and ask yourself: **"Without the thought, 'My soul is divine' who am I?"**

Example 3
My mind is driving me crazy.

Consider the payoffs then ask the feeling questions. Here are some sample answers:

I feel terrible—my mind won't stop.

I hate my mind for torturing me endlessly. If I could kill it, I would. I want my mind to be still. I want it to leave me alone.

Close your eyes and imagine that your mind is an object that is separate from you. Ask yourself:

"Without the thought, 'My mind is driving me crazy,' who am I?"

Your mind may continue to "think." If it does, just allow it. Ironically, the only painful thought is the thought that your brain shouldn't be thinking!

Give your mind permission to go on thinking endlessly for as long as it wants.

Believe it or not, you are not your mind. The brain's neurons fire—the brain "thinks"—and it calls itself "the mind." This is the brain's function as an organ of the body. Be kind to it and let it run if it wants to.

The FREE Process is essentially what happens in meditation. It is no different. Just recognize who you are without the thought that the mind shouldn't be doing what it is doing. Just contemplate:

"Without the thought, 'My mind is driving me crazy,' who am I?"

Example 4
My husband is mean to me.

Consider the payoffs then ask the feeling questions. Here are some sample answers:

I feel like a loser. I feel as if I'm not good enough, and my husband is better than me.

I feel disconnected from my husband. Separate. I stay away from him because I don't want him to hurt me. I treat him as a stranger, and I'm aloof. I want him to know what it feels like to be rejected.

I just want my husband to love me completely. I want him to be sweet to me and always want me in his life.

Now close your eyes. Imagine that your husband is in front of you, and ask yourself:

"Without the thought, 'My husband is mean to me,' who am I?"

Just sit with the answer, feeling, awareness, or nothingness as long as it feels comfortable.

Example 5
People shouldn't suffer.

Consider the payoffs and ask the feeling questions. Here are some sample answers:

I feel as if I could be doing more to help them, and I'm selfish. I feel awful for them.

I want the people of the world to have love.

I want them to have enough of the things they need to be healthy and happy. I want their suffering to stop.

Close your eyes, imagine suffering people in your mind's eye, and ask yourself: **"Without the thought, 'People are suffering,' who am I?"**

Just sit with the answer, feeling, awareness, or nothingness as long as it feels comfortable. Allow the mind to be active of not. There is no right or wrong feeling, or right or wrong "realization."

Example 6
I love Mike.

It's interesting to inquire into a thought that appears stress-free, natural, and loving.

Consider the payoffs and ask the feeling questions. Here are some typical answers:

It feels good, I love him dearly.

I treat him as if he's the most important thing to me. I don't want to be without him.

I really want to feel totally connected to him at all times. He makes me happy.

I want Mike to totally love me.

Close your eyes, imagine Mike or your object of love or pure desire in front of you. Ask yourself:

"Without the thought, 'I love Mike,' who am I?"

Just sit with the answer, feeling, or awareness.

Radical Truth

The FREE Process can be both radical and subtle. These examples are used to point out just how radical it can be. Be kind to yourself in the process, and use practices and techniques that work for you. We are just asking questions and finding answers. That's it. Very simple. No judgment—only honest answers that arise within. They are your answers and no one else's. Your answer to the exact same question may change moment to moment.

For example, to the question, "Without the thought, 'People shouldn't suffer' who am I?" A normal response is as quick as a hand moving away from fire. "No! No one should suffer."

If you can just ask, "Who am I without this thought?" a whole new awareness may be experienced. Your truth, your integrity may say, "No!—they definitely should not suffer." That is the perfect answer for you and to try to have a different answer in the moment you are inquiring lacks honesty and is not genuine. Be true to you. That is of the utmost importance. Right and wrong are concepts of the mind.

Allow the mind, body, and feelings to have whatever thoughts and reactions they may. No thought is higher or lower, more spiritual or more despised than any other. Just examine the thought and inquire: "Without it, who am I?" Transcendence and merger can happen at any moment no matter the prior thought, so be kind to yourself with whatever arises within.

It may seem extreme, but we are working on collapsing all sense of separation with objects, concepts, feelings, and beliefs. There is only oneness, love, and non-judgment in the field. All objects collapse into and merge with Source within you.

Our positive thoughts about love are also incredibly helpful to investigate. Through inquiry, we will experience that the object of our love and desire is not separate from us though the body, brain, and mind are usually convinced and programmed to believe that they are.

The FREE Process is designed to break down all sense of separation so that the object of each thought returns to the place from where it originates: you, your heart, your center—which is unconditional love itself.

The difficult thoughts, beliefs, and feelings that arise inside us are an intrinsic part of the human experience. Perhaps we can use the FREE Process to make peace with them. Rumi eloquently describes the reality that all sorts of thoughts, beliefs, and feelings arise day to day, but we don't have to greet them with pain, discomfort, or disdain. He reveals what is possible in his poem, "The Guest House," as translated by Coleman Barks:

> *This being human is a guest house. Every morning a new arrival.*
>
> *A joy, a depression, a meanness, some momentary awareness comes as an unexpected visitor.*
>
> *Welcome and entertain them all! Even if they're a crowd of sorrows, who violently sweep your house empty of its furniture, still, treat each guest honorably. He may be clearing you out for some new delight.*
>
> *The dark thought, the shame, the malice, meet them at the door laughing, and invite them in.*
>
> *Be grateful for whoever comes, because each has been sent as a guide from beyond.*

Without this thought... Who am I?

Martin Birrittella is an entrepreneur, inventor, artist, writer, and was the co-founder, chairman and CEO of two multi-million dollar companies he took public in 1988 and 1993. He retired from all business activities at age 41 to pursue his first love, meditation. He is a captivating storyteller and presenter. Having lived in India he also managed an ashram in Boston for four years in the late 70's. He has practiced meditation and self-inquiry for over 40 years. His theories and published works are on the cutting-edge of conscious thought philosophy. He attended Cornell University school of engineering, is a holder of multiple patents, and is a recognized self-taught and happily retired primitive naive artist. He is author of *Field of Love: Power, Love and Fortune on the Road to Enlightenment—A True Story*, *Field of Love: How to Experience the Field* and *Field of Love: Self-Inquiry and the FREE Process Workbook*. He is a gifted facilitator who loves to work with others and share his approach to the practice of self-inquiry. He lives in Sedona, Arizona.

Other Books by Martin Birrittella

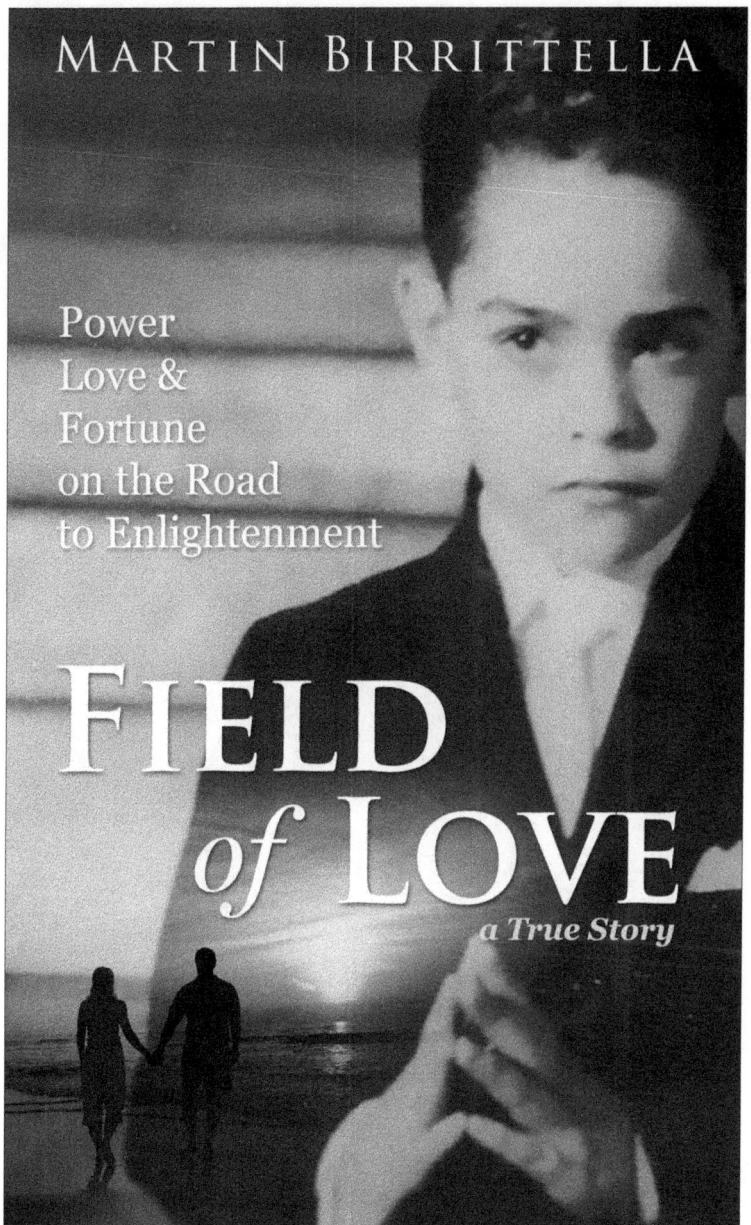

Field of Love
How to Experience the Field

THE FIELD

MARTIN BIRRITTELLA

Notes:

Without this thought... Who am I?

www.ingramcontent.com/pod-product-compliance
Lightning Source LLC
Chambersburg PA
CBHW060533030426
42337CB00021B/4233